Essential Life Science

THE HUMAN BODY

Melanie Waldron

Raintree is an imprint of Capstone Global Library Limited, a company incorporated in England and Wales having its registered office at 7 Pilgrim Street, London, EC4V 6LB – Registered company number: 6695582

www.raintreepublishers.co.uk
myorders@raintreepublishers.co.uk

Edited by Nancy Dickmann and Abby Colich
Designed by Rich Parker
Original illustrations © Capstone Global Library Ltd 2014
Illustrated by HL Studios
Picture research by Tracy Cummins
Originated by Capstone Global Library Ltd
Printed in China by China Translation and Printing Services

ISBN 978-1-4062-6225-4 (hardback)
17 16 15 14 13
10 9 8 7 6 5 4 3 2 1

ISBN 978-1-4062-6235-3 (paperback)
18 17 16 15 14
10 9 8 7 6 5 4 3 2 1

British Library Cataloguing in Publication Data
Waldron, Melanie.
  The human body. -- (Essential life science)
  1. Human body--Juvenile literature.
  I. Title II. Series
  612-dc23

Acknowledgements
We would like to thank the following for permission to reproduce photographs: Capstone Library: pp. 10 (Karon Dubke), 11 (Karon Dubke), 22 (Karon Dubke), 23 (Karon Dubke), 27 (Karon Dubke), 28 (Karon Dubke), 29 (Karon Dubke); Getty Images: pp. 5 (Cultura Science/Joseph Giacomin), 9 (Simon Gerzina Photography), 30 (Tim Hall), 32 (Rayman), 33 (Christian Gstöttmayr), 34 (Ambre Haller), 36 (Blend Images), 39 (Lena Granefelt), 42 (Ryan McVay); Istockphoto: p. 41 (© Denis Radovanovic); Photo Researchers, Inc.: pp. 6 (Scott Camazine / Science Source), 12 (Susumu Nishinaga / Science Source), 21 (Science Source Colorization by: Mary Madsen), 31 (Science Source/Jessica Wilson), 37 (Scott Camazine / Science Source), 38 (3D4Medical / Science Source); Shutterstock: pp. 4 (© Yuri Arcurs), 8 (© Kruglov Orda), 13 (© Morgan Lane Photography), 15 (© Asichka), 16 (© Aubord Dulac), 18 (© Pete Saloutos), 24 (© turtleman), 26 (© lev dolgachov), 40 (© wavebreakmedia), 43 (© Greg Epperson); Superstock: p. 19 (© Tetra Images).

Cover photograph of a woman doing a handstand on a mountain reproduced with permission from Getty Images (Paul Richer).

Every effort has been made to contact copyright holders of material reproduced in this book. Any omissions will be rectified in subsequent printings if notice is given to the publisher.

Contents

Eureka moment!

Learn about important discoveries that have brought about further knowledge and understanding.

DID YOU KNOW?

Discover fascinating facts about the human body.

WHAT'S NEXT?

Read about the latest research and advances in essential life science.

Some words are shown in bold, **like this**. You can find out what they mean by looking in the glossary.

Your amazing body

Imagine you were trying to design a robot that could do everything your body can. What would it look like? How would you programme it to do everything that your brain tells your body to do? It would be impossible!

Your body is amazing. Just think of all the different things you can do in a day – walking, jumping, climbing, or just reading this book. Think about all the tiny movements that are involved in even the simplest tasks.

DID YOU KNOW?

Some companies are spending millions of pounds on developing robots that can do basic human tasks. However, even taking a set of keys out of a pocket is too complicated for the most sophisticated robots!

Your body can move around in lots of different ways, and it can do lots of different things.

Think about it

If you had to think about every single thing your body did, you probably wouldn't do much at all! Your brain and your body work together to do countless different things without you even noticing. In this book we will find out what some of these things are.

What is my body made of?

Every part of your body is made up of **cells**. These tiny units are the basic building blocks of all life forms. There are many different types of cells, and they join together to do different jobs. For example, **muscles** are made up of millions of long, narrow cells.

Your body is working even when it is totally still. This image shows the heat that the body creates, using energy from food. We need to stay warm to stay alive.

How can my body move?

Under your skin you can feel your bones. Together they make up your skeleton. Your whole body is held up by your skeleton, which gives it structure, strength, and shape. Without your skeleton, your body would be a floppy pile on the floor. Your skeleton also makes it possible for you to move around.

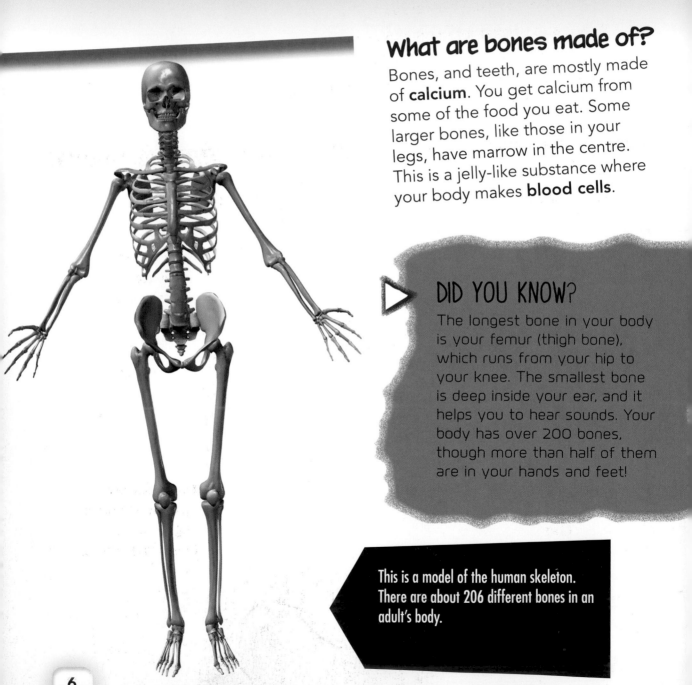

What are bones made of?

Bones, and teeth, are mostly made of **calcium**. You get calcium from some of the food you eat. Some larger bones, like those in your legs, have marrow in the centre. This is a jelly-like substance where your body makes **blood cells**.

DID YOU KNOW?

The longest bone in your body is your femur (thigh bone), which runs from your hip to your knee. The smallest bone is deep inside your ear, and it helps you to hear sounds. Your body has over 200 bones, though more than half of them are in your hands and feet!

This is a model of the human skeleton. There are about 206 different bones in an adult's body.

Where your bones meet

Joints are the places in your body where bones meet and connect together. There are different kinds of joints, depending on how the bones need to move, for example:

- hinge joints: these allow back and forward movements, like your knees

- ball-and-socket joints: these allow movement in all directions, like your shoulders

- pivot joints: these allow turning movements, like your neck.

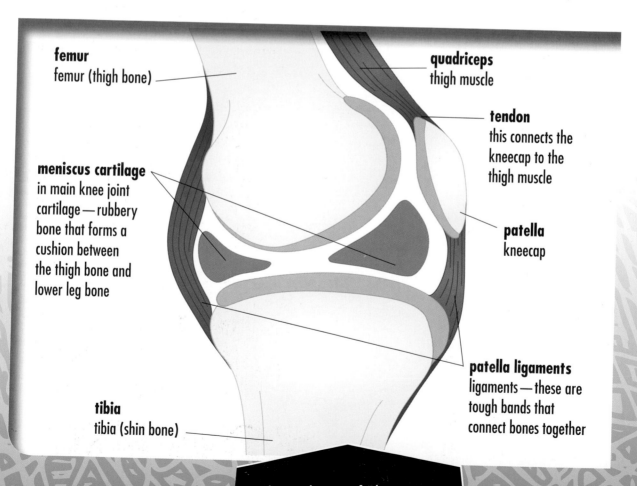

femur
femur (thigh bone)

quadriceps
thigh muscle

tendon
this connects the kneecap to the thigh muscle

meniscus cartilage
in main knee joint cartilage — rubbery bone that forms a cushion between the thigh bone and lower leg bone

patella
kneecap

tibia
tibia (shin bone)

patella ligaments
ligaments — these are tough bands that connect bones together

This is a diagram of a knee joint. You can see how the various parts are connected together.

What makes my joints move?

Your bones and joints can't move on their own. They need muscles and tendons to make the movements. Tendons are strong bands, which attach your muscles to your bones. Your muscles can contract – this means that they get shorter and tighter. They can also relax – this means that they get longer and looser.

When your muscle contracts, it pulls on the tendon and this moves the bone in one direction. A different muscle relaxes to let this happen. When you need to move the bone the other way, the first muscle now relaxes and the other one now contracts.

Gymnasts need to practice for a long time. This makes their bodies flexible enough to move into some amazing positions.

WHAT'S NEXT?

Many people, often athletes, injure their tendons. This is painful and can mean that they have to rest for a long time, to allow the tendon to heal before they can exercise again. Some scientists are trying to develop artificial tendons. These could be attached to the muscle and bone near the injured tendon, giving it support and helping it to heal quicker.

Other muscles

Not every muscle in your body is connected to bone. Different types of muscles do different jobs. Your stomach is surrounded by muscles that contract and relax to churn your food. Your heart is made of special muscles that pump your blood around your body. Your face is full of tiny muscles that work together to make all your expressions, such as smiling or frowning.

Anger, shock, happiness and lots of other emotions can be shown on your face using different facial muscles.

Try this!

You can do some simple experiments to demonstrate how amazing your body is. The activities below will show you how useful your joints and muscles are, even for the most simple tasks.

What you need

- wooden ruler
- tape
- objects to pick up

What you do

1 Lay a wooden ruler along the inside of your arm, over a long-sleeved top.

2 Tape the ruler in place, above and below your elbow. It might be easier to ask a friend to help you with this!

3 Now try to do a simple task using this arm. Try typing at a keyboard, for example. How difficult is it? Do you find you have to move other parts of your body, for example your shoulders, to get your hands in the correct places?

4 Now try to put something in your mouth. This will be impossible! Imagine if you had no joints in your arms. You would not be able to feed yourself.

Good grip

1. Tape one of your thumbs to the finger next to it. Again, it is probably easier if you ask a friend to help you do this.

2. Now try to pick something up with this hand – is this difficult? Which shapes are the hardest to pick up with this hand?

3. Work out how you can pick up an object that is a difficult shape. Do you need both hands? Could you use your feet? Can you see what an important joint the thumb joint is?

What fuels my body?

Your body needs energy to keep you warm, move around, grow, and repair. It gets this energy from food. Food contains lots of different chemicals that your body needs. These are called **nutrients**, and include **protein**, **carbohydrates**, **vitamins**, **minerals** like calcium, and fats.

Getting nutrients from food

Your body has to **digest** the food you eat to get at all those nutrients. The first part of this process happens in your mouth. Your teeth chew the food. Your body makes a liquid called saliva, which contains chemicals that help break down the food. Your tongue mixes the food and saliva then pushes it to the back of your mouth.

This is part of a tongue, magnified under a microscope. You can see that the surface is not smooth. This helps it to grip the food you are chewing.

Swallow it down

Once your mouth has chewed your food, your throat swallows it and pushes it into a tube called the **oesophagus**. This is connected to your stomach. Muscles in the oesophagus push the food down into your stomach.

Your stomach contains liquids called gastric juices. These contain chemicals, which dissolve the food into liquid and help the nutrients get released.

WHAT'S NEXT?

Apples are not only delicious and healthy, they could save lives too! Scientists have discovered a chemical – also in oranges and onions – that can help to prevent **blood clots** inside the body. This chemical could be used to prevent heart attacks.

It is important to eat a wide variety of healthy foods. Each type of food contains a different mix of nutrients.

The job of intestines

After the food has been churned into a liquid by your stomach, it passes into a long, coiled tube called the **small intestine**. As the food passes through this, the nutrients in it are **absorbed** by tiny hair-like strands.

After passing through the small intestine, the remains of the food pass into the **large intestine**. Here, your body absorbs water from the food. Your intestines are also known as your bowels.

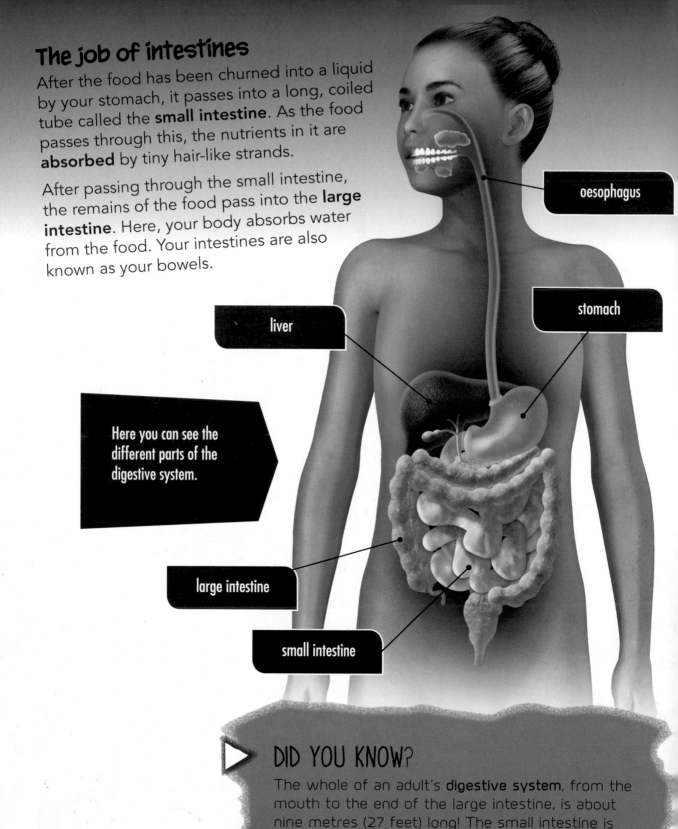

Here you can see the different parts of the digestive system.

oesophagus

liver

stomach

large intestine

small intestine

DID YOU KNOW?

The whole of an adult's **digestive system**, from the mouth to the end of the large intestine, is about nine metres (27 feet) long! The small intestine is about four times longer than the large intestine. It is called the small intestine because it is much thinner than the large intestine.

What is my liver?

Your liver is a large **organ** that sits just next to your stomach. All the chemicals that your intestines absorb go to your liver. There, they are sorted out and sent to the parts of your body that need them. Your liver stores some chemicals for your body to use later. It also traps chemicals that might harm your body, and breaks them down to make them less dangerous.

Your body needs water to work properly. Make sure you drink enough!

WHAT'S NEXT?

Turmeric, a spice used in cooking, contains a chemical called curcumin. Doctors have known for many years that this chemical helps to prevent bowel **cancer**. Now they are doing trials to see if it can be used to treat people who already have bowel cancer.

How does my body deal with waste products?

Your body does not need every part of the food you eat. The leftover bits are waste products that your body needs to get rid of.

In your large intestine, the waste products mix with tiny living things called **bacteria**. They form brown lumps called faeces. Faeces pass down to the bottom end of your large intestine, called the rectum. They are stored there until you go to the toilet. The faeces then pass through the anus, which opens up to let it pass.

▷ DID YOU KNOW?

Your intestines contain billions of bacteria – but don't worry, they are mostly friendly bacteria! They help your body to absorb important vitamins. They also feed on the undigested food, reducing the amount of waste your body needs to get rid of.

After you have been to the toilet, make sure you wash your hands really well. This is to make sure that none of the bacteria from inside your intestines spread to things you touch.

Kidneys and urine

Your two **kidneys** clean your blood as it passes through them. Waste chemicals and water are removed from your blood and made into **urine** (wee). Urine is stored in your **bladder**, until you are ready to go to the toilet.

WHAT'S NEW?

People suffering from kidney failure must spend long hours hooked up to machines, which clean their blood. However, scientists are developing artificial kidneys to do the same job. The artificial kidney is strapped to the waist, and patients can go about their daily lives while it cleans their blood.

This diagram shows your body's **urinary system**.

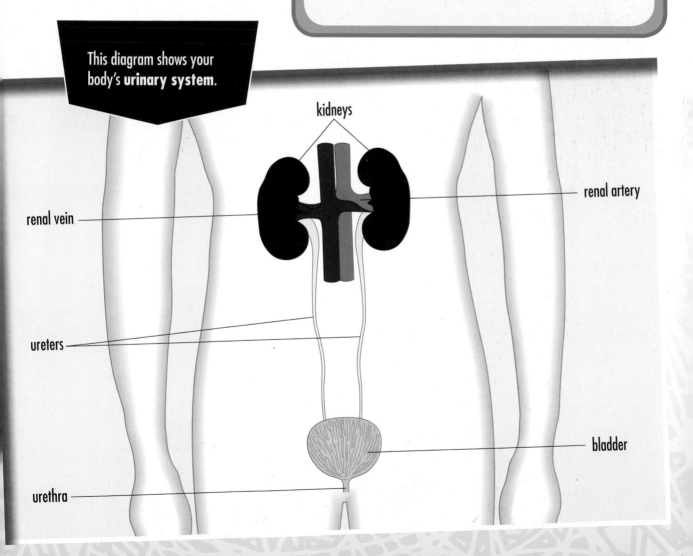

kidneys

renal artery

renal vein

ureters

urethra

bladder

What do my heart and lungs do?

Every minute of every day, your heart beats. All day and night you breathe air in and out of your lungs. Your heart and lungs work together to keep the right amount of oxygen in your body. Oxygen is a gas found in the air and it is essential for staying alive – cells in your body need oxygen to help them get energy from nutrients.

Your lungs

When you breathe in, air is sucked into your mouth or nose and down into a pipe called the **trachea**. This is connected to your lungs. Your lungs are full of tiny little air sacs, like a sponge. These are called **alveoli**.

When you run fast, your body needs a lot of oxygen. You need to breathe faster and more deeply to get enough oxygen into your body.

Eureka moment!

In 1928 doctors in the USA invented the iron lung. This is a machine that helps people to breathe when they are unable to do so on their own. The first iron lungs looked like metal coffins. People would lie in them with just their heads sticking out. The pressure inside the iron lung would decrease and increase, making air flow into and out of the lungs.

Exchanging gases

The walls of the alveoli are very thin, and oxygen from the air you have breathed in passes through them and into your blood. At the same time, a waste gas called carbon dioxide passes from your blood into your lungs. When you breathe out, you get rid of this carbon dioxide.

The air you breathe out contains carbon dioxide.

How does my blood move around?

Once your blood has got its oxygen from your lungs, it needs to travel all around your body, delivering the oxygen to where it is needed. It travels along tubes called blood vessels. Blood vessels that carry blood away from the heart are called **arteries**, and those that carry blood towards the heart are called **veins**.

Eureka moment!

William Harvey was an English doctor. In the early 1600s he did some experiments on dead bodies, to try to work out how blood moved in the body. He realised that the heart was responsible for pumping the body's blood around in arteries, and that veins carried blood back to the heart.

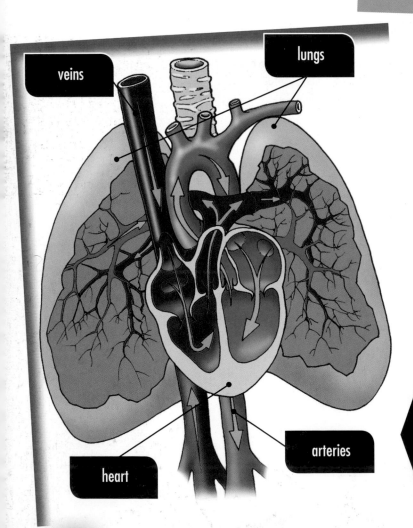

veins

lungs

heart

arteries

Your heart is the pump that provides the power to push your blood around your body. As it beats, it contracts, and this pushes the blood along. Your heart has two sides. One side pumps the blood to your lungs. The other side pumps the blood around your body.

This illustration shows the heart and lungs and the arteries and veins that carry blood to and away from them.

What else is in blood?

Your blood carries lots of important chemicals around your body, as well as oxygen and nutrients from food. It gets its red colour from **red blood cells**, which carry the oxygen. It also has **white blood cells**, which attack germs and diseases. **Platelets** in your blood can make the blood sticky and form scabs when you cut yourself.

This is what your blood looks like when it is magnified. The red discs are red blood cells.

Try this!

Your breathing rate is the number of breaths you take every minute. Your pulse rate is the number of times your heart beats every minute.

Prediction

My breathing rate and pulse rate will be low when I am resting. They will both increase as I move around. They will be highest when I am doing hard exercise.

What you need

- stopwatch
- some paper
- pencil

What you do

① Sit down. Relax and try to stay very still for a few minutes.

② Use the stopwatch to time a minute. Count how many times you take a breath in this minute. Write this down – this is your resting breathing rate.

③ Now measure your pulse rate over a minute. Find your pulse by holding two fingers to the inside of your wrist. Write your resting pulse rate down.

4 Now stand up and walk around the room, or outside, for a few minutes. Repeat steps 2 and 3, measuring your breathing rate and your pulse rate. These are your active rates. Write them down.

5 The next step is to do some hard exercise – perhaps jumping up and down, or skipping, or running if you are outside. Do this for at least three minutes. As soon as you stop, measure your breathing rate and pulse rate again over a minute. Write these down – these are your exercising rates.

6 Look at your breathing rates and pulse rates you have written down. Is the hypothesis correct?

What are my senses?

Your body has five **senses**, and they tell you about your surroundings. They can warn you of danger and help keep you safe! Your five senses are sight, hearing, smell, taste, and touch.

Seeing is believing

You use your eyes for sight. Light enters your eye through the little black hole in the centre. This is called the pupil. The light then passes through a clear pad called the lens. This changes shape so you can focus on things at different distances from you. The light then ends up on the back wall of your eyeball, called the retina.

The **iris** of the eye is the coloured part around the pupil.

WHAT'S NEXT?

Some blind people can have special **implants** put into their retinas, to help them see again. These have to be powered by little batteries which sit behind the ear. Scientists are now developing sunglasses that can send solar power from sunlight straight onto the implant, so there will be no need to link the implant to a battery.

Hear this

Your ears are what you use for hearing. Sound waves travel into your ear and down the **ear canal**. They hit the **eardrum**, and this begins to vibrate. Three tiny little bones deep in your ear start moving, and this moves a liquid inside the **cochlea**, which looks like a tiny snail shell. Tiny hairs inside the cochlea send signals to your brain, and you hear the sound!

This diagram shows the parts of your ears. Most of them are deep inside your head!

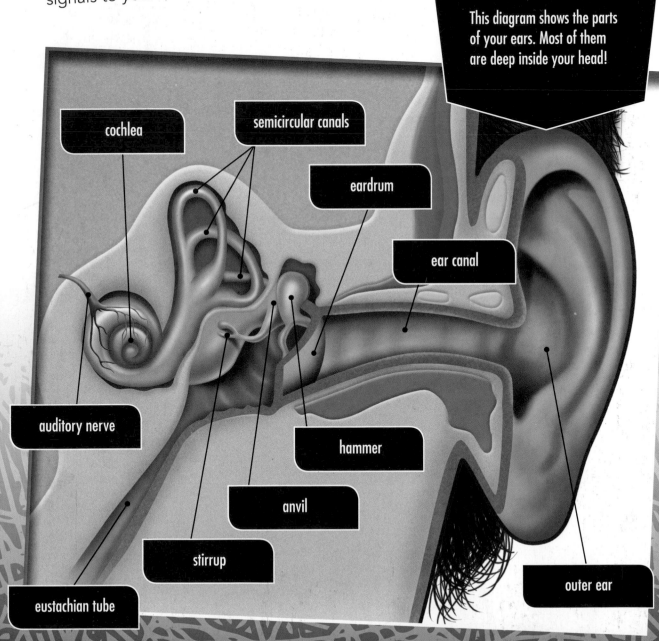

cochlea

semicircular canals

eardrum

ear canal

auditory nerve

hammer

anvil

stirrup

eustachian tube

outer ear

How do I smell and taste?

You use your nose to smell things. Smells are carried as tiny particles in the air. They enter your nose when you breathe in, and they hit tiny hairs called cilia inside your nose. Cilia can detect lots of different smells.

You use your mouth, especially your tongue, to taste things. Your tongue is covered in thousands of little **taste buds**. Taste buds detect different tastes in food: sweet, salty, sour, and bitter. Taste is linked to smell. Often, part of what you taste is actually smell.

Eureka moment!

In 2008, scientists discovered that people can actually smell fear. They gathered sweat samples from the armpits of terrified skydivers and asked volunteers to smell the samples. The volunteers had their brains scanned during the experiment, and scientists noticed that areas in the brain that are to do with fear became stimulated.

Our sense of smell can protect us! When something smells really bad, it is often a warning not to eat or drink it.

Touch and feel

You use your skin for your sense of touch. Just below the surface of the skin there are lots of **nerve endings**. These detect different things, like heat, cold, pain, light touch, and heavy pressure. Some parts of your skin have more nerve endings than others, and so are more sensitive to touch. Your fingertips, lips, and toes are the most sensitive areas on your body.

Your fingers are very sensitive to touch. You can tell what many things are, just by touching them. You would not be able to do this with your elbow!

Try this!

How sensitive are my fingers compared to other parts of my body?

Prediction

The sense of touch in my fingers is better than the sense of touch on my arm.

What you need

- blindfold
- friend to work with
- lots of things that feel different but are similar shapes – choose items that are soft; hard; rough; smooth; and everything in-between! For example, you could use: an orange; a stone; a big cotton wool ball; a tennis ball; an apple; a ball of play dough; an egg – the possibilities are endless!

What you do

1 One of you needs to decide who will wear the blindfold. Put this on carefully and make sure you can't see!

2 The blindfolded person should sit in a chair and roll up one sleeve, so the skin on the arm is visible. The other person should pick up an object, one at a time, and touch the arm with it.

3 The blindfolded person needs to try to guess what the object is. The other person should record how many times the blindfolded person gets the answer right.

4 After all the objects have been used, the blindfolded person should now try to guess what each object is by handling it with his or her fingers. The other person should hand him or her one object at a time, and again record how many times the correct answer is given.

5 Now look at the two sets of results. Did the blindfolded person correctly guess more objects using the skin on his or her arm or using his or her fingers?

6 Now repeat the experiment, swapping places so that you both get a turn to guess the object. Compare your results. Are they similar?

How does my brain control my body?

Your brain is your body's control centre. All day and night it is at work, receiving messages from all over your body and sending messages back. Your brain is a very complicated and mysterious organ – even today scientists don't completely understand how it works.

Your brain is more sophisticated than any computer. It can help you do lots of things at once, while at the same time keeping your body working perfectly and keeping you alive!

Creating connections

Every time you learn something new, like riding a bike, your brain makes new connections between different brain cells. The next time you get on the bike you find it a little easier, because the connections you made earlier are still there.

Different areas of the brain

Your brain is made up of areas that are responsible for different things. The main part is called the **cerebrum**. This is responsible for things like moving, thinking, and speaking. Your memories are stored all around your brain.

This model shows different parts of the brain. If part of a person's brain is damaged, for example the part that controls speech, he or she may lose the ability to talk.

cerebrum

corpus callosum

midbrain

thalamus

hypothalamus

pituitary gland

brain stem

cerebellum

What is my nervous system?

Your brain needs to be connected to the rest of your body in order to send and receive messages. Your **nerves** provide these connections. Your nervous system is the huge network of nerves that link all parts of your body. You have thousands of kilometres of nerves in your body!

Your spine contains the main bundle of nerves in your nervous system. This is called the spinal cord. All of the nerves that run to your legs, your arms, and the rest of your body branch out from the spinal cord.

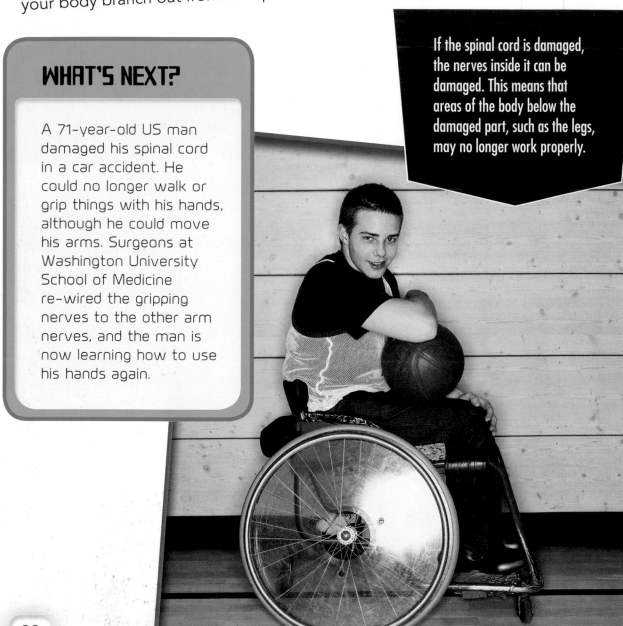

WHAT'S NEXT?

A 71-year-old US man damaged his spinal cord in a car accident. He could no longer walk or grip things with his hands, although he could move his arms. Surgeons at Washington University School of Medicine re-wired the gripping nerves to the other arm nerves, and the man is now learning how to use his hands again.

If the spinal cord is damaged, the nerves inside it can be damaged. This means that areas of the body below the damaged part, such as the legs, may no longer work properly.

Reflexes

Sometimes your body needs to react quickly to something, without you having to think about it. Your nervous system has **reflexes** to do this. These are simple actions that you sometimes can't control – like coughing if something catches in your throat.

Newborn babies have a grasp reflex. If you stroke the palm of a baby's hand, it will quickly close the hand into a grasp.

How does my body fight disease and infection?

Every second, your body is defending you against germs. Germs are tiny living things, like **viruses** and bacteria. They can get into your body and make you ill. Your body's **immune system** helps to defend you against germs.

No way in!

Your skin is part of your immune system. It covers your body, keeping germs out. If you breathe germs into your lungs, they get trapped in a sticky liquid called mucus. Tiny hairs push the mucus up into your throat. When you swallow, the mucus goes into your stomach. Your stomach attacks germs with **acid**, and there is more mucus in your intestines to trap any germs that manage to get through.

Other body substances fight germs too. Earwax helps to keep germs out of your ears, and chemicals in saliva and tears attack germs in your eyes and mouth.

Your skin stops many germs from getting into your body.

Eureka moment!

Louis Pasteur was a French scientist. In the 1850s, he discovered that bacteria made wine, beer, and milk go sour. He worked out that heating and then cooling the liquids killed the bacteria. This process is called pasteurization, and it is still used today to keep food and drink fresher for longer.

When you cut yourself, white blood cells leak out of your blood vessels to attack any germs that might enter you body.

Fighting germs

Some germs manage to get past your body's outer defences, and can get into your blood and body parts. White blood cells can attack and kill many of these germs.

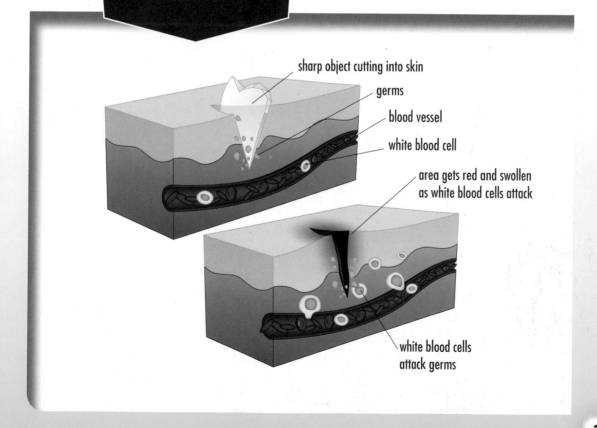

sharp object cutting into skin

germs

blood vessel

white blood cell

area gets red and swollen as white blood cells attack

white blood cells attack germs

What are diseases?

Sometimes germs get past your body defences, and can cause illness and disease. Other diseases, like cancer, happen by themselves inside the body, when some cells stop working properly and cause problems. Some illnesses can be treated and cured with medicines.

Some illnesses can be prevented from happening, with **vaccines**. Vaccines are medicines that make the body produce chemicals called **antibodies**. Antibodies stay in the body, ready to attack the germs that cause these illnesses.

Vaccines can keep you healthy and stop you from getting deadly diseases.

Eureka moment!

In 1796, a doctor called Edward Jenner made a vaccine for a terrible disease called smallpox. He took germs from a mild disease called cowpox, and put them into a cut on an eight-year-old boy's arm. A few weeks later, Jenner put smallpox germs into the boy. The boy did not develop smallpox, because the cowpox had made his body produce antibodies that kill cowpox and smallpox. The first vaccine had been made!

What are allergies?

Sometimes your body defences can react very strongly to something that is not actually very harmful. This is called an allergy. People can be allergic to many different things, including nuts, eggs, wasp stings, and cat hair. Hay fever is an allergy to **pollen** – from flowers and trees. It can make your eyes red and itchy, and your nose runny.

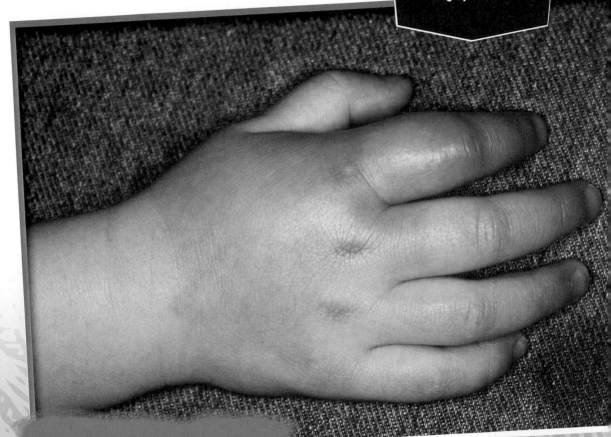

This girl's hand has swollen after being stung by a bee.

DID YOU KNOW?

Some people are allergic to very strange things, including water, sunlight, touch, and cold temperatures. Usually, the allergy produces red, painful lumps on the body called hives.

How do I grow and stay healthy?

From the time you are a newborn baby until adulthood, your body needs to grow and change. But before you were born, you had to be made! Babies are made when an egg cell in the mother joins up with a sperm cell from the father. This means that the egg is **fertilized**, and can now grow into a baby.

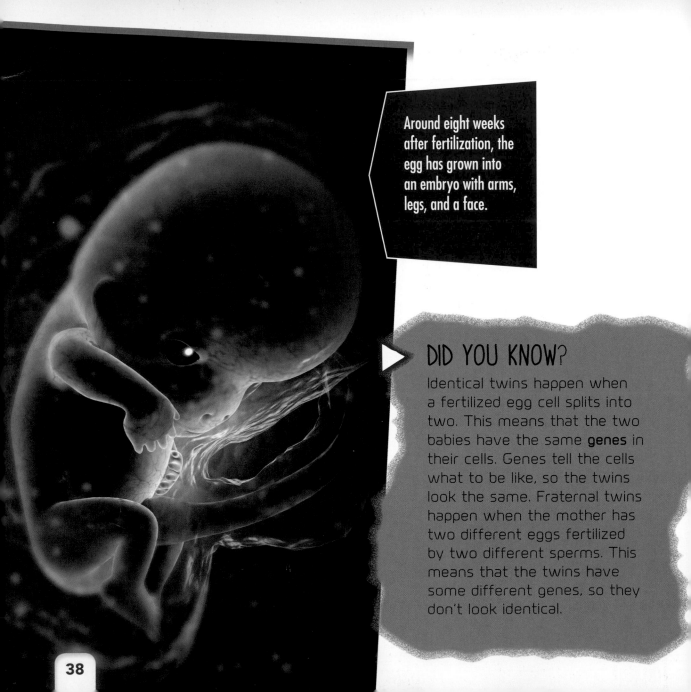

Around eight weeks after fertilization, the egg has grown into an embryo with arms, legs, and a face.

DID YOU KNOW?

Identical twins happen when a fertilized egg cell splits into two. This means that the two babies have the same **genes** in their cells. Genes tell the cells what to be like, so the twins look the same. Fraternal twins happen when the mother has two different eggs fertilized by two different sperms. This means that the twins have some different genes, so they don't look identical.

Growing babies

After about eight weeks, the fertilized egg has grown into a tiny human called a foetus. The foetus gets all its food and oxygen from the mother, through a tube called the umbilical cord. This attaches at the foetus's bellybutton.

After about 40 weeks inside the mother, the foetus has grown into a baby and is ready to be born. When it is born, the cord is cut and the baby must breathe and eat for itself. For a few months it can only drink milk, and then it can start to have more solid food.

Feeding yourself is just one of the many things you had to learn as a baby.

How can I take good care of my body?

To help your body grow properly, stay healthy, and get energy, you need to eat the right food! Eating a wide variety of different food will help to make sure you get as many different kinds of nutrients as possible. For example:

- Protein: you need this to help you grow and repair damaged cells. Meat, eggs, and nuts have lots of protein.

- Carbohydrate: you need this to give you energy. Bread, pasta, and breakfast cereals have carbohydrates.

- Fat: you need a little fat in your diet to give you energy, and help your body absorb some vitamins. Butter and cheese contain fat.

- Vitamins and minerals: there are lots of different vitamins and minerals. They do many different jobs, like keeping your bones strong, boosting your immune system, and making red blood cells. Fruit and vegetables contain different vitamins and minerals.

Learning to make tasty and healthy meals can be fun!

Move your body!

Exercising your body is another good way to stay healthy. Exercise can be anything, from going for a walk to playing a team sport. There is such a huge variety of exercise types, there really is something to suit everyone.

DID YOU KNOW?

Some foods have such good health benefits that they have been called "superfoods". Superfoods for children include blueberries, tofu, tomatoes, Greek yoghurt, cabbage, salmon, cocoa, black beans, basil, and cinnamon. Add them to your family's shopping list!

When you exercise, your body releases chemicals called **endorphins**, which can make you feel happy.

What have I learned about my body?

Your body is an amazing natural machine. It grows from a bundle of cells into a complicated factory where lots of things happen all the time. Your body does thousands of things automatically without you even noticing.

There are over seven billion people in the world, and we all look different on the outside. But we are all the same underneath, and our bodies all work in the same ways.

You have lots of different systems inside your body, all working together to keep you alive and healthy. Your skeleton, muscles, and joints keep you upright and moving. Your digestive system processes your food and gets rid of waste. Your heart and lungs work together to deliver oxygen around your body. Your senses keep you informed about your surroundings. Your nervous system relays messages to and from your brain, which controls everything!

Doing amazing things

We can use our bodies to do amazing things. Our brains can think of complicated ideas and solve tricky problems. We can use our brains and hands together to create beautiful pieces of art and practical tools.

We can't rely on our bodies to take care of themselves though – we have to help out. We need to eat well, exercise, and drink enough water. We also need to make sure we get enough sleep, so that the brain and the body can rest and recover.

When we keep our bodies and brains fit and active, we can do some incredible things, like this rock climber.

Glossary

absorb take in or soak up

acid chemical substance. Stomach acid dissolves food.

alveoli air sacs in the lungs

antibody part of the blood that reacts to disease to protect the body. Antibodies stay in the body so they are ready in case the same disease reoccurs.

artery blood vessel that carries blood away from the heart

bacteria microscopic organisms. Most are useful because they help our bodies to, for example, digest food. Some can cause disease though.

bladder organ inside the body that collects urine (wee)

blood cells cells in the bloods that carry oxygen (red blood cells) or help to fight infection (white blood cells)

blood clot thick lump of blood. Blood clots in the body can lead to heart attacks.

calcium nutrient that can be found in cheese and milk. It is important for building healthy bones and teeth.

cancer disease in which certain cells divide and grow much faster than they normally do

carbohydrate nutrient found in food such as cereals and bread. Carbohydrates are important for giving us energy.

cell tiny part of human or plant life

cerebrum largest part of the brain, which controls movement and thinking

cochlea spiral tube in the inner ear, containing nerve endings that help us to hear

digest to break down food into materials that can be used by the body

digestive system parts of the body that work together to break down food so that it can be used by the body as energy. The human digestive system includes the mouth, oesophagus, stomach, and intestines.

ear canal part of the ear that leads from the outside to the eardrum

eardrum part of the ear inside the head that receives sounds

endorphins chemical released by the brain that can make us feel happy or relaxed

fertilize in the human body, when the sperm cell from the male joins with the egg cell from the female. Once fertilized, the egg cell can develop into a foetus.

genes parts of the body that we inherit from our parents. Genes cause particular characteristics, such as eye or hair colour.

immune system body's system of organs, tissues, and cells that protect the body against disease and infection

implants something placed in the body by surgery

iris coloured circle around the pupil of the eye

kidneys organs in the body that remove water and waste products from the blood

large intestine part of the body where water is absorbed from food, and solid waste matter is formed

minerals substance that we get from food. Some minerals are important for keeping us healthy

muscle bundle of fibres that move the body by tightening and relaxing

nerve fibre that carries messages between the brain and other parts of the body

nerve ending part of the nerve with which we feel things that we touch

nutrient substance in food that our bodies use to live and grow

oesophagus tube that moves food from your mouth to your stomach

organ part of the body that performs a particular task. The heart, the lungs, the skin, and the eyes are all organs

platelets small disc-shaped parts of the blood that help blood to clot

pollen fine yellow powder made by a flowering plant

protein nutrient that we can get from food such as eggs, meat, and beans. Protein is important for helping our bodies to grow and fight disease.

red blood cells cells that carry oxygen around the body

reflex automatic reaction that we do not have to think about

senses ways in which we understand our surroundings. The five senses are sight, hearing, smell, taste, and touch.

small intestine part of the body that connects the stomach and the large intestine. It is where food is broken down and nutrients absorbed into the blood.

taste buds bumps on the surface of the tongue that tell us whether something is sweet, sour, salty, or bitter.

trachea (windpipe) tube in the body that carries air to the lungs

urinary system parts of the body that work together to produce urine and get rid of it

urine yellow liquid (wee) that is made by the kidneys to carry waste products from the body

vaccines germs of a disease that are dead or not active. Vaccines are injected into people to help their immune system protect against the disease.

vein blood vessel that carries blood towards the heart

viruses tiny organisms that can cause disease in the human body

vitamin substance in food needed to keep our bodies working and healthy.

white blood cells cells that help the body to fight infection and disease

Find out more

Books

First Encyclopaedia of the Human Body, Fiona Chandler (Usborne, 2011)

Human Body: An Interactive Guide to the Inner Workings of the Body, Steve Parker (Natural History Museum, 2010)

The Children's Book of Healthy Habits, Sophie Giles (Award Publications, 2011)

The Human Body Factory, Dan Green (Kingfisher, 2012)

Websites

www.bbc.co.uk/schools/ks3bitesize/science/organisms_behaviour_health/life_processes/revise1.shtml
This BBC Bitesize site has a lot of information about the human body and the processes that go on inside it to keep us alive and healthy. There are lots of activities and tests too.

www.fankids.org/
Fankids is a website all about food allergies. It gives information about all kinds of food allergies, and advice on living with a food allergy.

kidshealth.org/
If you go to the "Kids site" part of this website, you will find all sorts of useful information. There are movies, quizzes, activities, and articles, which will help you learn more about your body.

www.sciencemuseum.org.uk/broughttolife.aspx
The Science Museum has a section on its website which is all about the history of medicine. You can find out how treatments and hospitals have changed through the ages, and all about the people, equipment, and technology used in the development of medicine.

science.nationalgeographic.com/science/health-and-human-body/human-body/
This National Geographic website contains lots of interactive diagrams, full of information about various parts of the body.

Organizations to contact

WHO

www.who.int/en/

The World Health Organization is concerned with all sorts of health matters around the world. It encourages research into staying healthy, monitors health around the world, and improves people's access to treatment for illnesses.

Save the Children

www.savethechildren.org

This organization saves the lives of children around the world. They promote and provide better healthcare for children in poor countries.

Places to visit

The Science Museum in London has galleries devoted to the history of medicine, how your brain works, and understanding health and disease. You can see some objects from the past related to medicine.

ThinkTank, Birmingham's Science Museum, has lots of fun interactive galleries including one all about the human body. You can play with a giant digestive system! There is another gallery all about medicine and you can perform a virtual hip operation.

Further research

There is a lot more information about the human body you could find out about. What interests you most about it? Do you want to find out more about how the brain and nervous system work? Are you interested in learning how doctors can treat illnesses?

Index